PHILLIP MARGULIES

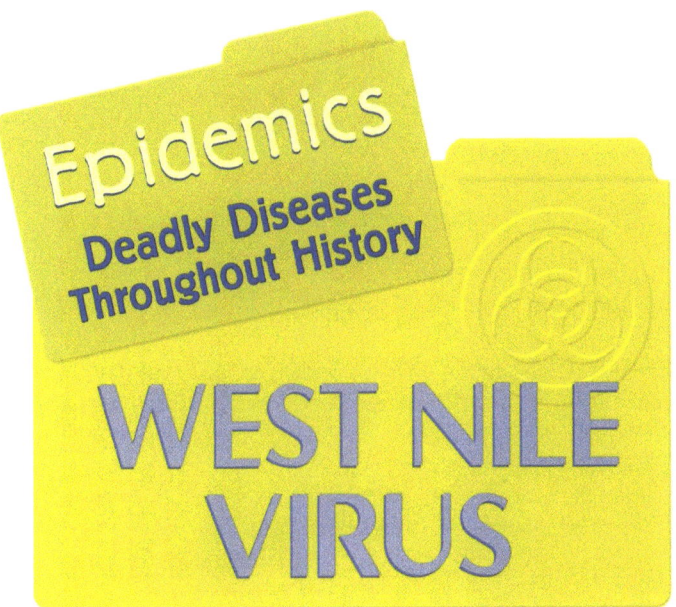

Epidemics
Deadly Diseases Throughout History

WEST NILE VIRUS

The Rosen Publishing Group, Inc.
New York

Published in 2004 by The Rosen Publishing Group, Inc.
29 East 21st Street, New York, NY 10010

Copyright © 2004 by The Rosen Publishing Group, Inc.

First Edition

All rights reserved. No part of this book may be reproduced in any form without permission in writing from the publisher, except by a reviewer.

Library of Congress Cataloging-in-Publication Data

Margulies, Phillip.
West Nile virus / by Phillip Margulies.
   p. cm. — (Epidemics)
Summary: Looks at the disease known as West Nile fever caused by West Nile virus, tracing its history to the present and predicting its future.
ISBN: 978-1-4358-3652-5
1. West Nile fever—Juvenile literature. 2. West Nile fever—United States—Juvenile literature. 3. West Nile virus—Juvenile literature. [1. West Nile fever. 2. West Nile virus. 3. Diseases.] I. Title. II. Series.
RA644.W47 M37 2003
616.9'25—dc21

2002153884

Manufactured in the United States of America

Cover image: A transmission electron microscope (TEM) view of the West Nile Virus

CONTENTS

	Introduction	5
Chapter 1	A Killer	9
Chapter 2	The History of West Nile Virus	15
Chapter 3	West Nile Virus in America	26
Chapter 4	The Science of West Nile Virus	39
Chapter 5	Battling the Virus	46
	Glossary	54
	For More Information	57
	For Further Reading	59
	Index	60

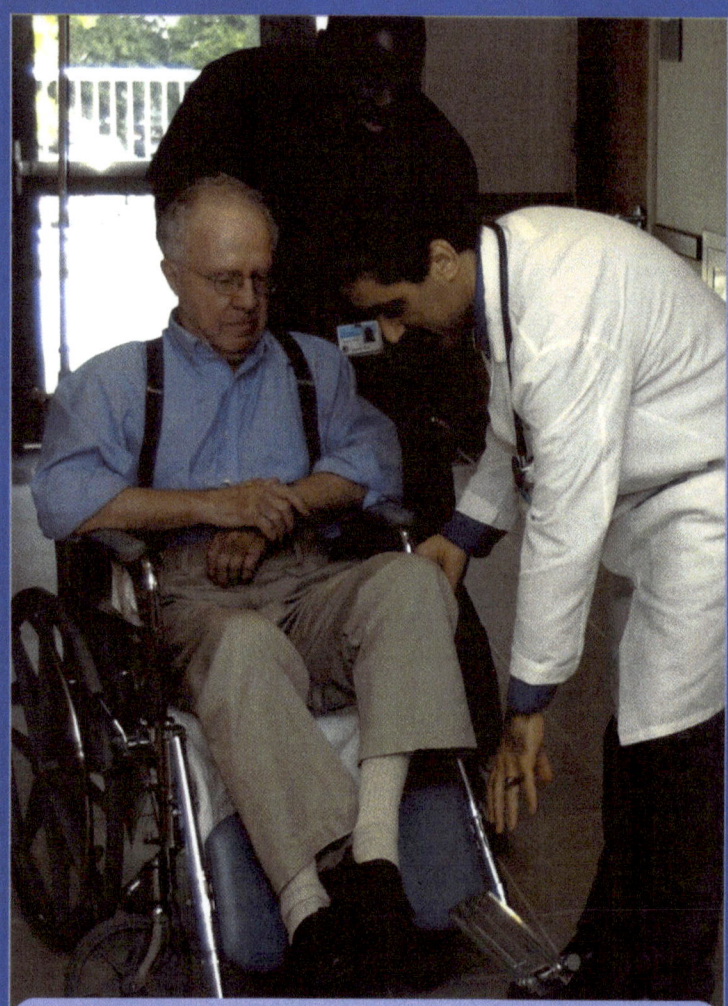

Americans first became infected with mosquito-borne West Nile virus in 1999, which caused a public health scare in some areas.

INTRODUCTION

The West Nile virus is native to Africa and has existed there, infecting people and wildlife, for thousands of years. But in the 1990s, it traveled beyond the borders of its native land. It arrived in Romania in the summer of 1996 and in America in the summer of 1999. By spreading to continents where it had never been before, it became what scientists call an emergent virus, or a virus that has broken out of its old home.

Emergent viruses are unpredictable. A virus that has found a new home can be much more dangerous than it was in its native land because people and animals in the virus's new home may have less resistance to the virus than those in its original home. This is because the immune systems of people who have not been exposed to a particular type of virus have not had the chance to build up enough strength to fight it. The result is that more people become sick, making the epidemic more devastating.

Other conditions that keep the virus under control in its original environment may not work in its new environment. Responding to its new environment, the virus may even change form. This would make it more harmful, because when a virus changes form, the immune system that has already built up defenses against it will not recognize it. As a result, it will not know how to fight this new strain. In effect, the new strain is almost like a new virus altogether.

Since viruses become more dangerous when this happens, medical authorities worry a great deal about viruses that become emergent. Throughout history, emergent viruses have been infamous for their devastation, causing death and destruction within entire societies. This can be seen in a short history of one of the major emergent viruses of the sixteenth century.

When the Spanish conquistadors arrived in Central America in the 1500s, they had tools that gave them enormous advantages over the peoples of the New World. Their steel armor, guns, and horses made them more powerful than any society the world had ever seen. And so, the mighty empire of the Aztecs fell before a handful of Spanish soldiers.

INTRODUCTION

But without knowing it, the Spanish brought something far more deadly to America than their weapons: they carried the disease smallpox. Smallpox killed most of the people it came into contact with. The people who survived were left disfigured by ugly scars. However, by this time most Europeans were immune to the disease because it had already existed in Europe for centuries. The Europeans had had time to develop defenses against it.

Native Americans, however, had no immunity to the disease. We don't know which Europeans first passed on the virus to which Native Americans, but whenever it happened, it led to one of history's greatest human catastrophes. In 1518, the population of the Aztec Empire, where Mexico is today, was 30 million. By 1568, an estimated 3 million remained. Native Americans called it the "Great Dying."

These days, with jet travel linking every continent and country, there are more emergent viruses than ever before. We can't know in advance which of them will turn out to be the new epidemic, but when a virus appears in a new place, health experts go into high gear, scurrying to contain it before it has a chance to show what it can do. Considering that health care today is far superior than it was back in Central America in the 1500s, viruses have to be far stronger to cause the kinds of problems smallpox did.

But while new medicines are coming out every day, viruses are growing stronger and more resilient to them. In effect, the viruses are outsmarting us. The story of the West Nile virus is the story of one of these new epidemics and the efforts of a handful of people to stop it in its tracks.

A KILLER

In August 2002, a killer was on the loose in southeastern Louisiana. It had already been found in thirty-eight states across the nation. Seven people were dead, victim to its activities since June, and its rampage had only just begun. It would kill 188 people before the year was over. This killer was invisible. It could travel in the body of human being or in the body of a bird or an insect. It could be in many places at once, though it preferred to strike in certain kinds of places and at certain times of day, especially early in the morning and at twilight.

People turned on the news to hear warnings that sounded desperate, as if the region were at the mercy of a bloodthirsty maniac. People were told to stay indoors at dawn and at dusk and to replace torn screens in doors and windows so the killer couldn't get in. They were also told to wear clothes that covered their arms and legs and to wear mosquito repellant when they went outside.

The killer of course was the West Nile virus, and it entered the human body through the bites of infected mosquitoes. If the killer had been a man, slaying seven people and showing no signs of stopping, the FBI would have gotten together with local law enforcement to hunt him down and bring him to justice. But since the killer was a virus, the job fell to the Centers for Disease Control and Prevention (CDC).

From CDC headquarters in Atlanta, Georgia, and from its Division of Vector-Borne Infectious Diseases in Fort Collins, Colorado, came a quickly assembled "fever team" of specialists to work in an empty building at Slidell Memorial Hospital, a hospital in Louisiana that had seen most of the state's West Nile virus patients so far that year. They worked in a wide first-floor office with cafeteria tables shoved against the walls. The room was full of computers, phones, and file cabinets. Its walls were covered with maps, lists of phone numbers, and patient charts.

The head of the team was Mike Bunning, a forty-seven-year-old epidemiologist, a person who studies

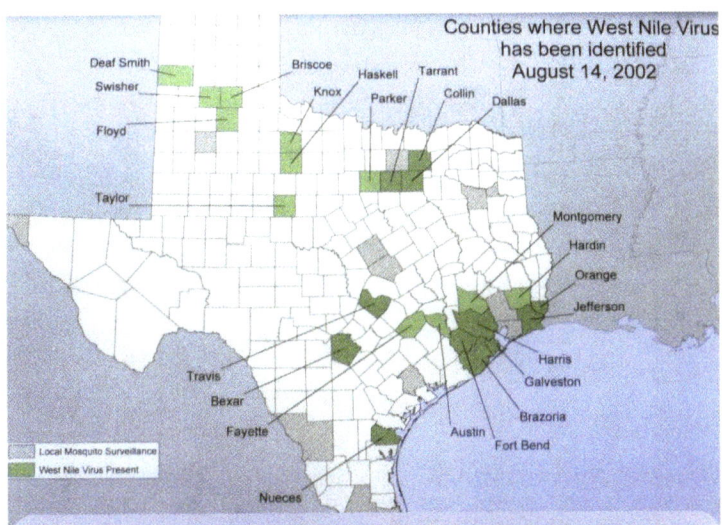

This map from the Texas Department of Health shows counties in Texas that were affected by an outbreak of West Nile virus during the summer of 2002.

the way diseases spread. Bunning was also a veterinarian and U.S. Air Force officer who had investigated the first West Nile virus outbreak in New York in 1999 as well as the mysterious anthrax attacks in the autumn of 2001. Other members of the team included epidemiologists Stacie Marshall from Colorado and Judy Krueger from Atlanta; doctors Ann Buff from Tulane University and Kwame Asomoa, who were also from Atlanta; Ellie Click, a fourth-year medical student from Stanford University; and technician Aaron Kipp.

The team's goal was to locate the mosquitoes carrying the virus. In this way they hoped to establish a more targeted effort to eliminate the epidemic. Whenever they figured out that someone had gotten the disease from a mosquito bite in a certain place, they noted it on the map. The places where the virus showed up were known, in the language of epidemiology, as the hot zones.

The Obstacle

The biggest problem to the fever team's efforts to find the hot zone was the fact that the West Nile virus had a relatively long incubation period—between three and fourteen days would pass between the time someone was bitten by a virus-carrying mosquito and the time the victim got recognizably sick.

Also, the West Nile virus traveled fast. In addition to humans, it infected birds, which meant that it could travel untracked by way of infected birds. And what's worse, birds, unlike most animals, tend to migrate over long distances. This meant that not only would the birds spread the disease over a large area, they would also bring the disease to places where people did not have an immunity to it. By the time West Nile virus was known to have struck in one place, it had already moved on, and the new hot zone was somewhere else. "We are looking for a needle in a haystack," Bunning admitted.

A KILLER

A National Scare

West Nile virus was a top news story across the country in the late summer and fall of 2002. Health authorities reminded people to be alert but not to panic. After all, they reminded the public, most people who were infected by the West Nile virus would not even know it because they wouldn't become ill at all. About 20 percent of the people who became infected developed only West Nile fever, a relatively mild illness with flulike symptoms, including fever, headache, and body aches. In some of the relatively mild cases of West Nile fever, there would be a skin rash on the trunk of the body and swollen lymph glands.

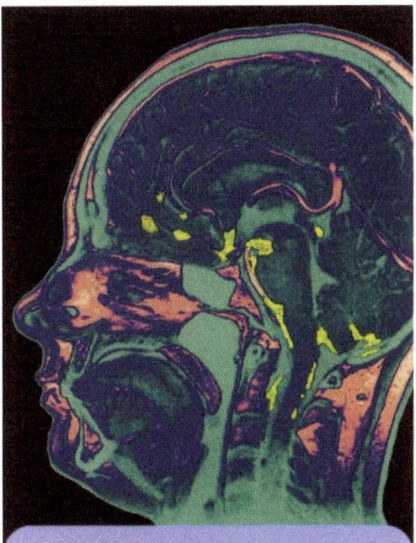

A magnetic resonance imaging (MRI) scan of a woman's head, in which meningitis is shown in yellow.

Only one in 150 of those infected would develop the severe form of the disease, known as West Nile encephalitis or meningitis, the symptoms of which are inflammation in the brain or spinal column. (This condition is called encephalitis when it affects the brain, meningitis when it affects the spinal column, and meningoencephalitis when it affects both.) The symptoms of encephalitis also include headache, high fever, neck stiffness, stupor, disorientation, coma, tremors, convulsions, muscle weakness, and paralysis. Many West Nile encephalitis victims die, and many of those who do not die suffer permanent brain damage.

The scariest thing about the West Nile virus wasn't the damage it did, as bad as that was for the handful of people who came down with the serious form of the fever—many other diseases do far worse damage and kill many more people every year. The scary thing about the West Nile virus was that it was something new to North America, which made it exceptionally dangerous. No one could know for sure then—or even now—how serious a threat the West Nile virus might pose in the future. What they did know was that as time passed, the outbreaks were becoming more serious, causing widespread illness and killing more people.

THE HISTORY OF WEST NILE VIRUS

Scientists first learned of the West Nile virus in 1937 when they were studying an entirely different disease. The disease was African trypanosomiasis, commonly known as sleeping sickness. Sleeping sickness is a very serious affliction that kills about 55,000 people every year—around 150 people every day—in Africa. It also harms African agriculture, making cattle lean and sickly.

Sleeping sickness has an important place in the history of medicine. It was one of the first vector-borne infectious diseases discovered by science. Vector-borne diseases get their name from the way they infect people. We come down with colds and flus from direct exposure to people who have the illnesses. We get their germs from a sneeze or from touching something

VECTOR-BORNE INFECTIOUS DISEASES

A research scientist examines mosquitoes to be tested for the West Nile virus.

The CDC classifies the West Nile virus as a "vector-borne infectious disease," because it is spread by insects that feed on both animals and human beings. Some of the deadliest diseases in the world have been vector-borne. The bubonic plague, which killed a third of the population of Europe in the fourteenth century, was a vector-borne disease spread by a deadly combination of rats and fleas. Rats were the "reservoir" of the virus, carrying it in their bodies, and fleas were the means of transmitting it to human beings. Even though people knew that the plague was contagious, and therefore stayed away from people who had it, they still got sick from the bites of fleas.

Mosquitoes, which carry the West Nile virus, are a very common vector for diseases. Around the world, five hundred people are infected by mosquito-borne diseases every year. Each year, almost three million people infected by mosquito-borne diseases die.

they've put their germs on. The illnesses are spread "person to person." By contrast, vector-borne diseases aren't spread from person to person. Instead, people get vector-borne diseases through a go-between, usually an insect. The go-between is called the vector.

Since sleeping sickness takes such a toll on the people of Africa, it has been the subject of intense study. In 1937, researchers conducting a sleeping sickness study traveled to the Ugandan village of Omago to get blood samples to study the prevalence of the disease. They took a blood sample from a thirty-seven-year-old woman who had a temperature of 100.6° (38.1°Celsius) Fahrenheit but who said she did not feel sick. The researchers took the sample back to a clinic in Entebbe, Uganda, and injected it into ten mice. Nine of the mice died. When healthy mice were given blood samples taken from the sick mice, the healthy mice died as well. Dr. K. C. Smithburn and his team knew they were looking at a new virus, but they did not know how the woman had become infected with it.

Later on, other researchers found that the virus had infected animals in many parts of Africa and the Middle East. In the 1940s, the virus was found to be especially widespread in the Nile River region of Egypt and acquired the name of West Nile virus after the West Nile region of Uganda, where it was first found. Virus researchers already suspected that it was vector-borne: People did not get it from each other but from the bites of mosquitoes. Mosquitoes became infected with the virus when they sucked the blood of birds and animals, and later on they passed it to human beings. In 1943, animal experiments confirmed this guess.

The Virus Spreads

There are a great many viruses in the world. Though they're all of some scientific interest, most of them don't seriously harm human beings and don't affect our lives very much. Back in the 1940s, the West Nile virus seemed like one of them. It was relatively rare among human beings, and when it did show up it appeared to do less harm than the common cold.

The view that the West Nile virus was a rare and relatively harmless disease began to change during a series of outbreaks in Israel in the 1950s. During these outbreaks several elderly people came down with severe forms of either encephalitis, meningitis, or meningoencephalitis.

Over the years, the West Nile virus continued to spread. A small outbreak occurred in southern France in 1962, and a much larger one occurred in South Africa in 1974. The South African epidemic occurred

Ron Abernathy, an employee of Rob Reed Pest Control, Inc., sprays pesticide on trees in Roswell, New Mexico, to help stem the tide of the expected arrival of West Nile virus.

after unusually heavy rains in the Capetown area. Since mosquitoes breed in puddles, researchers believe the rains probably led to a temporary increase in the number of mosquitoes, which carried the disease, and led to increased infection. Around three thousand cases of West Nile fever turned up in Capetown clinics and hospitals during the 1974 epidemic. Researchers now believe that South Africa's 1974 epidemic was caused by a different and less dangerous strain of the virus than the one that later spread across North America. The strain of the virus we are seeing in the United States is much more likely to cause serious illness and death.

University of Florida student Barry Alto shows reporters the backpack aspirator, which helps researchers and government officials collect mosquitoes for further study.

The Virus Hides

Viruses have a way of disappearing and reappearing, especially those, like the West Nile virus, that prey on many different species. The virus can hide for years in the bodies of animals before showing up again among human beings. It multiplies and is spread by mosquitoes that carry it between different animals. The virus may also infect human beings but not make any of them sick enough to cause an investigation that would identify the virus. In any event, there were only a few scattered cases of the virus reported between the mid-1970s and the mid-1990s. Over the course of twenty years, the virus was almost forgotten.

The Virus Changes

But when the West Nile virus came back, it was different. It reappeared in the 1990s in Europe, Asia, and North America as a stronger and more dangerous virus. Epidemiologists Lyle R. Petersen and John T. Roehrig, looking at the recent history of the virus, noted some "disturbing trends." Since the mid-1990s, they observed, there has been an increase in the frequency of West Nile virus outbreaks. And the number of people with the most severe form of the disease is rising with each outbreak.

Romania, 1996

The first of the large epidemics that announced the return of the West Nile virus occurred in Romania, between July and October of 1996. The outbreak was the worst in Bucharest, the capital city of Romania, and on the plains around the Danube River.

The Romanians realized they had an epidemic on their hands in August, when unusually large numbers of patients started appearing in their hospitals with infections of their central nervous systems—that is, with

1937
Uganda
The West Nile virus is first found in a woman in the West Nile region of Uganda. Scientists realize they have found a new virus but do not yet know how it is spread.

1950
Israel
Earliest reported epidemic occurs with more than 500 clinical cases (cases serious enough for people to seek medical attention). By now it is known that mosquitoes spread the virus. The first cases that cause encephalitis appear.

1974
South Africa
The largest human epidemic of West Nile virus breaks out in Cape Province, South Africa. Thousands of clinical cases are noted.

meningitis and encephalitis. There were 835 of these patients in hospitals in Bucharest. According to an investigation conducted later, 762 of them had symptoms of West Nile fever. Most of the remainder probably had the virus as well but didn't happen to be textbook

THE HISTORY OF WEST NILE VIRUS

1996
Romania
The virus seems to have mutated into a more dangerous form. 762 confirmed cases; 17 deaths.

1999 July to October
Russia
480 confirmed cases in the Volgograd region of the Russian steppe; 40 deaths.

2002
United States
The most deadly outbreak of the West Nile virus to date. 3,391 cases in 38 states and the District of Columbia; 188 deaths.

1999 July to October
United States
First appearance in North America. 62 clinical cases in the New York City area; 7 deaths.

2002 July to October
United States
First reported case of West Nile Virus being passed from mother to child before birth.

cases of the disease. Thus, more than 800 people had the severe form of West Nile fever. No one could know for sure how many people had milder cases, which had not been serious enough to bring them to the hospital. Seventeen people died in the Romanian epidemic.

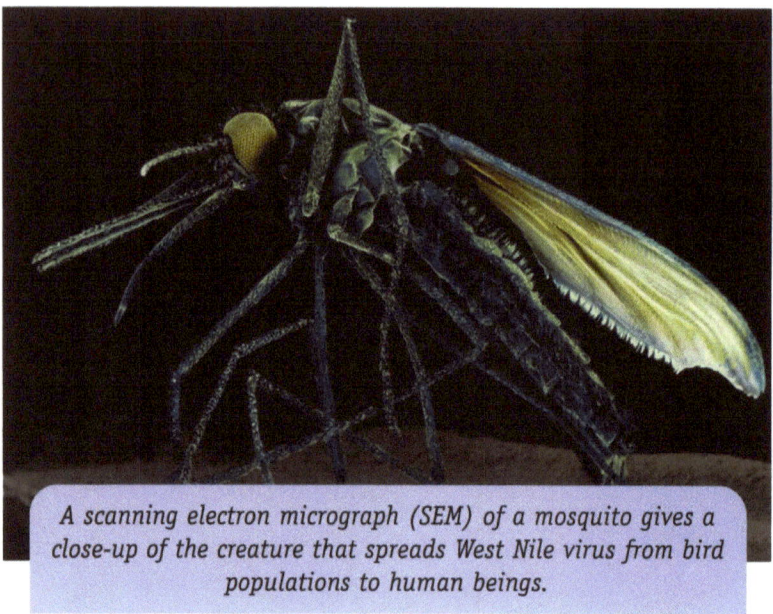

A scanning electron micrograph (SEM) of a mosquito gives a close-up of the creature that spreads West Nile virus from bird populations to human beings.

Scientists who later reported on the Romanian epidemic in the British medical journal the *Lancet* said that the disease was probably spread in Bucharest by the mosquito *Culex pipiens*, also known as the common house mosquito, throughout many of the apartment blocks and houses in the city and countryside.

Russia, 1999

The next large outbreak of the West Nile virus in Europe occurred in 1999, again between July and October, in the Volgograd region in the Russian steppe (plains). The city of Volgograd has a population of one million. Like Bucharest, it is located on the bank of a famous river—in this case, the great Volga River. The city of Volzskii, with a population of three hundred thousand people sits on the opposite bank of the river.

From July 25 to October 1, 826 patients were admitted to the hospital in the area with symptoms that included meningoencephalitis, meningitis, and acute viral infection with fever. There were 480 confirmed cases of West Nile virus. As in the case of the Romanian epidemic, there were probably many more cases than were confirmed. Most of the patients were at least fifty years old. Forty of the patients died.

That same year, for the first time, the West Nile virus appeared in North America.

WEST NILE VIRUS IN AMERICA

In August 1999, health officials noted an increase in the number of dead birds in New York State, especially crows. Ward Stone, a wildlife pathologist in Albany, began receiving the crows' bodies in the mail, sent for his inspection by puzzled local health authorities. He received more than a hundred of these dead birds. He cut them open and tested their tissues to see if they had been poisoned by something they ate. Maybe they had suffered from lead poisoning. Maybe a pesticide had killed them. But the tests did not turn up any evidence of poison. Could it be a new disease? Stone sent samples of the birds' tissues for analysis to specialized labs, including the National Veterinary Services Laboratory in Ames, Iowa.

Ward Stone, a wildlife pathologist, inspects a crow for signs of West Nile virus at a Department of Environmental Conservation laboratory in Delmar, New York.

Some of the crows sent to Stone had been found near the grounds of the Wildlife Conservation Society in the Bronx Zoo. In early September, staff at the zoo found that whatever had killed the crows had spread to the zoo's own exotic birds, which were sick and behaving strangely. A cormorant, a kind of waterbird, spent its last hours swimming in circles. A bald eagle had tremors. The illness killed the cormorant, two Chilean flamingos, and an Asian pheasant. Veterinary pathologists (doctors who study disease in animals) dissected the dead birds and found they had had encephalitis and myocarditis. Tissues from these birds were also sent to the lab in Ames, Iowa.

Meanwhile, John Andresen, a private veterinarian on Long Island, was answering calls from people whose horses were sick or behaving strangely. One horse was found collapsed and thrashing in a field. Another walked with its head tilted and leaned against a fence as if trying to keep its balance. Another tripped over its own hind legs. As more horses in his area came down with illness, Andresen called the state veterinarian to report the mystery.

The Virus Strikes Humans

Reports of the same sickness in human beings began in late August 1999. A doctor from a hospital in northern Queens, New York, found two patients with encephalitis. Unable to determine the cause and concerned about an epidemic of a new disease, the doctor notified the New York City Department of Health and Mental Hygiene (NYCDOHMH). The NYCDOHMH began an investigation, making calls to other hospitals in the area, and found a total of six patients with encephalitis. The patients' blood was tested for virus. The NYCDOHMH concluded that they had come down with a new strain of St. Louis encephalitis, a virus that has been found in North America since 1933. The NYCDOHMH was mistaken, but it was an understandable mistake. The St. Louis encephalitis virus is a

A cloud of pesticide follows in the wake of a municipal truck enlisted to poison the mosquito population of Fort Wayne, Indiana, after a West Nile-infected crow was found dead the previous week.

close relative of the West Nile virus. They are both spread by mosquitoes.

Believing that they were combating a potential epidemic of St. Louis encephalitis, New York City began spraying pesticides to kill mosquitoes in Queens. When a man in Brooklyn came down with encephalitis, the spray program was expanded to include the whole city.

Finally, in the third week of September 1999, the CDC began to connect the dots between the sick animals and the sick humans. Testing on the dead birds' tissues and the brain tissue of a human encephalitis case both revealed the presence of the West Nile

Fire department emergency medical technician Ray Rodriguez gives out insect repellant to the public in the College Point section of Queens, a New York City area particularly affected by West Nile.

virus. From what was known about the behavior of the virus in other parts of the world, it was obvious that mosquitoes were carrying the disease between birds and humans.

In New York City, on the advice of the CDC, the mosquito spraying continued. Emergency telephone hot lines were set up to answer people's questions about the outbreak and the spraying. By September 28, around 130,000 calls were received by the New York City hotline. Around 300,000 cans of mosquito repellant were distributed in New York City through local firehouses, and 750,000 public health leaflets were distributed with information about protection against mosquito bites. Public messages about the epidemic were announced on the radio, on television, over the Internet, and in newspapers.

By late October, the outbreak had run its course. According to public health authorities, there were 62 cases of severe West Nile virus in hospitals during the 1999 outbreak. Seven of the patients died. Doctors investigating the outbreak suspected many more people might have been infected. Knowing this for certain was important. The answer would tell them how widespread the virus was, and it might also tell them how often it was deadly. If the West Nile virus was behaving as it usually did, it had infected many more people than it made seriously ill.

Investigators could not test everybody in New York for the virus. There were simply too many people to test. But they could test a random sample of people from different households in the region to get an idea of what percentage of them might have been infected with the virus. Asking for volunteers, the doctors took blood samples from 677 people in 459 households in the areas. Of the volunteers, 2.6 percent tested positive for the virus. Based on this sample, investigators concluded that between 3,500 and 13,000 people in the New York area had been infected with the West Nile virus. The good news was that most of these people had not become seriously ill—in fact, most of them had not even noticed that they were infected. The bad news was that the virus was already very widespread, and it was probably in North America to stay.

The West Nile Virus in 2002

For two years the West Nile virus lay relatively low in North America, just doing enough damage to warn us that it had not gone away. In 2000, twenty-one human cases of encephalitis caused by the West Nile virus were reported, and there were two deaths. In 2001, there were fifty human cases, and five deaths.

Then, between July 2002 and October 2002, the virus struck as it had never struck anywhere before. It killed more people than ever. The fever teams of the CDC struggled to track the virus and contain the epidemic.

What made the 2002 outbreak so bad? One answer is probably the heat. Researchers noticed that the virus seemed to be at its worst during hot, dry summers, which may have promoted the breeding of mosquitoes. The summer of 2002 was one of the hottest and driest on record. But another reason the 2002 outbreak was so bad was that the West Nile virus had spread so far during the relatively mild 2000 and 2001 seasons. It had been detected in four states in the 1999 outbreak, but it was found in thirty-eight states in the 2002 outbreak.

Initially, in July and August, the highest number of serious cases was found in the Deep South, in Louisiana, and the CDC sent its best team of specialists to Slidell Memorial Hospital in St. Tammany Parish to track the virus. But the virus outwitted its human hunters. In the end it turned out that the heaviest concentrations of cases and deaths were in the Midwest. Illinois was hit the worst, with 714 cases and 45 deaths caused by the West Nile virus. Michigan had 463 cases and 36 deaths. In Louisiana, where 317 cases were reported, 16 people died.

In all, in July through October 2002, 3,391 people died in the United States from illness caused by the West Nile virus, more than in any other recorded outbreak. The numbers were discouraging to public health workers and local governments. They had worked hard to fight the virus, and they had worked with advantages they didn't have in the first outbreak. They had known the virus was in the United States. They had studied its history in other countries, and they had known a great deal about how it was spread. They had known that it started to strike birds and humans in July. They had known the best way to combat the virus was to control the breeding of mosquitoes, and they had launched programs to educate the public about mosquitoes and to spray mosquitoes wherever the virus was suspected of

Mark Baker, chief of field operations for the Northwest Mosquito Abatement District, checks a catch basin for mosquito larvae in Niles, Illinois, in August 2002.

being. Still the virus had done more damage than it had ever done before and struck in a greater area than ever before.

St. Louis Encephalitis

Some epidemiologists believe it is possible to learn about the future of the West Nile virus by looking at its close relative, St. Louis encephalitis. St. Louis encephalitis got its name from the city in which it first appeared in 1993. It is found only in North and South America. Since 1964, there have been 4,478 reported human cases of St. Louis encephalitis in the United

WEST NILE VIRUS IN THE BLOOD SUPPLY

You cannot get the West Nile virus from sharing an elevator or a drinking glass with someone who has it. It has to find its way directly into your blood. A bite from an infected mosquito is the way that people usually get the West Nile virus, but it can happen another way. West Nile can be transmitted during a blood transfusion. In the 2002 outbreak, a handful of people got the West Nile virus this way.

To understand how this can happen, it helps to know a little about the uses of donated blood. When patients in hospitals have lost blood because of a wound or because they have had surgery, they are given donated blood to make up for the blood they've lost. This blood is donated by people to blood banks all over the country and shipped to hospitals. It is sorted according to blood type, since people need to have blood of their own type, and it is also separated into various special blood products such as red blood cells and plasma (blood serum without blood cells) to be given to people according to their medical needs. In addition to testing for type, donated blood is tested for some especially dangerous and widespread viruses, such as HIV. (In fact, many people contracted HIV from blood transfusions before the blood supply began to be tested for HIV.) But it is not possible to test donated blood for every virus.

In the summer of 2002, the CDC began to receive reports of cases in which people had come down with the West Nile virus after receiving blood transfusions in hospitals. Investigators found that some of those who had given blood later came down with the West Nile virus. Since the virus has a fifteen-day incubation period and some people who

(Continued on page 36)

WEST NILE VIRUS IN THE BLOOD SUPPLY *(Continued from page 35)*

are infected never become ill, people can unknowingly pass it along.

The CDC shares responsibility for the safety of the blood supply with the Food and Drug Administration (FDA). Together, they are dealing with the problem of keeping the blood supply free from West Nile. The CDC is tracking down the infected blood. The FDA is working with researchers for public institutions and private companies to develop a West Nile virus test that could be used to screen blood. Meanwhile, the CDC stresses that the risk of getting the West Nile virus from a blood transfusion is very low, and the benefits of blood transfusions far outweigh the risk.

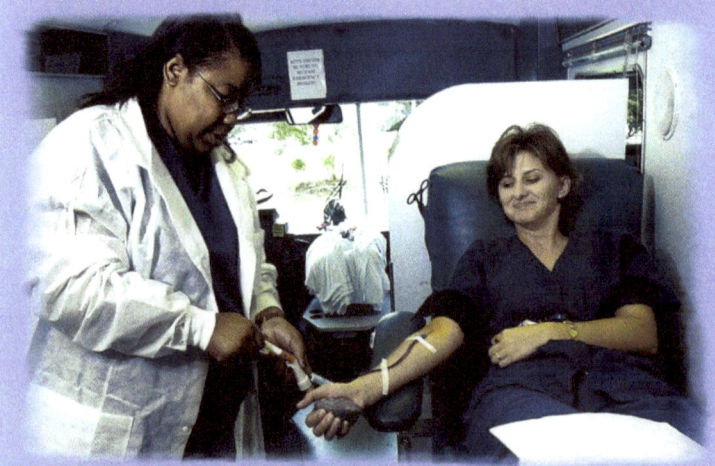

A technician at United Blood Services in Vicksburg, Mississippi, empties a blood sample. In 2002, a few people contracted West Nile virus by receiving blood transfusions.

States. Each year on average, 128 cases are reported, according to the CDC. The last major epidemic of St. Louis encephalitis occurred in the Midwest from 1974 to 1977. More than 2,500 cases were reported in 35 states. Since the late 1970s, though, there have been no major outbreaks of St. Louis encephalitis. A handful of people get the disease each year.

When the West Nile virus appeared in New York City in 1999, public health authorities at first mistook it for St. Louis encephalitis. This was understandable—the West Nile virus and St. Louis encephalitis are close cousins. Both are classified by biologists as belonging to the same family of viruses. They have many of the same genes and symptoms. Outbreaks tend to occur in summer and early fall, as with West Nile virus, and people catch both of the viruses in the same way: Mosquitoes become infected by feeding on birds infected with the virus. However, there are important differences as well. Unlike the West Nile virus, St. Louis encephalitis doesn't cause sickness in birds or mosquitoes—they are simply carriers of the disease. That means there's no dying off of birds to warn health authorities that an outbreak of St. Louis encephalitis should be expected. And a victim of St. Louis encephalitis actually runs a greater risk of death than someone with the West Nile virus. While only one out of every 150 cases of West Nile virus is serious, between 3 and 30 percent of people who get St. Louis encephalitis die.

Some scientists predict that the West Nile virus will eventually follow the pattern of St. Louis encephalitis. Sally Slavinski, an epidemiologist for the Mississippi Department of Health thinks so. Speaking in August 2002, she said, "Next year, we probably will see some West Nile activity, but hopefully not to the same degree, if we can use St. Louis as a model."

4

THE SCIENCE OF WEST NILE VIRUS

Viruses are the smallest and simplest organisms known. Though scientists have been aware of their existence since the late nineteenth century, viruses were far too small to be visible under the microscopes that medical researchers used to look at tiny one-celled organisms such as bacteria. Not until the invention of the electron microscope in the 1940s was it possible to see viruses.

How do viruses manage to be so small, yet do so much damage? Viruses don't have to be able to survive on their own—they live only in other organisms. All other living things are made of cells, each of which has its own special equipment for eating, turning food into energy, and reproducing. Viruses get along without that equipment. They get the cells of other living things to do their work for them, so they don't carry the baggage other living things need to carry in order to do their daily business. They are stripped down to their very basics. A virus consists of only what is necessary to invade a cell in the body of another organism and a set of instructions that tells the invaded cell what to do. The virus instructs the cell to make copies of the virus. The cell then makes copies of the virus until the cell bursts.

The Immune System v. the Virus

Most of the time, the human immune system is very good at fighting viruses. Our bodies recognize a virus as an alien invader and make special killer molecules called antibodies to fight them. Often we get sick anyway because creating antibodies to fit a particular virus takes time. In general, the time it takes to make the antibody for a new viral infection accounts for the length of time we're sick with the illness.

We usually don't get sick from the same virus twice, and this is why: After we recover, our immune systems keep a few copies of the antibody to use in case the infection returns. If the same virus comes again, the immune system recognizes it and makes many copies of the antibodies for that virus. This time the immune system has a head start on the virus. It knocks the virus out so quickly we aren't even aware of it. Not only is this why we don't usually get sick from viruses we've already gotten, it is also what permits doctors to develop vaccines against viruses. Vaccines help us develop the antibodies for a virus in advance, without making us ill.

The most dangerous viruses are those, like the Ebola virus, that kill very quickly, before antibodies for them can be developed, or like the HIV virus, which disables the immune system altogether.

The West Nile Virus and Its Family

The West Nile virus is one member of a family of related vector-borne viruses around the world called flaviviruses, which are similar to each other in their structure and their behavior. St. Louis encephalitis is another member of this family. So is the virus that causes dengue fever, a disease that kills hundreds of people every year in tropical regions, and the virus that causes Japanese encephalitis, which results in an estimated fifty thousand cases and ten thousand deaths a year, mostly in Asia and Indonesia.

The West Nile virus itself comes in a variety of different strains, since, like other viruses, the West Nile virus changes over time. The forms of the virus that have been causing outbreaks in recent years are different from the forms that were originally found in Africa. Among these various new strains of the West

PESTICIDE DEBATE

In the summer of 1999, New York City responded to the threat of the West Nile virus by spraying mosquitoes with the insecticide malathion in Brooklyn, the Bronx, and Queens. The following summer the choice of pesticide was switched from malathion to a product that went under the commercial name of Anvil. To former New York City mayor Rudolph Giuliani and the New York Department of Health, spraying with one pesticide or another was the obvious course of action.

But was it? Not everyone thought it was a good idea to spread pesticide all over the city. After all, pesticide is poison. It kills butterflies and many other beneficial insects as well as mosquitoes. And it has long-term effects on human health that are difficult to measure. Since the risk of the West Nile virus is very low, many argued that spraying urban areas with pesticide does more harm than good.

Controversy raged over the safety of malathion and Anvil. According to Mayor Giuliani, "You have to virtually . . . drink Anvil in order to have side effects," and he called people who questioned the use of pesticides "environmental terrorists," who "like to get you angry because it gets them on television."

But all pesticides pose some risk to human health. Malathion is a toxic nerve gas. Anvil can cause asthma and has been linked to breast cancer. Ironically, many of the same people who tend to get serious cases of the West Nile virus—the very young, the very old, and those with weakened immune systems—are the most likely to be hurt by pesticides.

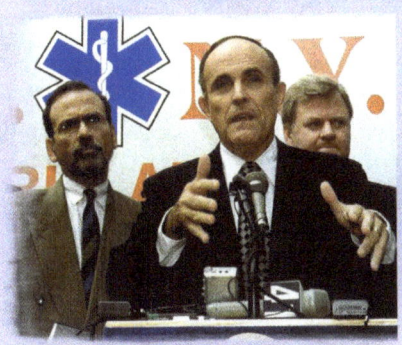

Former New York City mayor Rudolph Giuliani sparked controversy when the city combated the West Nile virus with mass pesticide spraying.

There were also debates about the way the spraying was done. Opponents said that the warnings on the labels of the pesticides were being ignored. Spraying was being done directly on humans, and over bodies of water, without giving enough warning to people in the neighborhoods where it was used, and not at the best time for killing mosquitoes. Some said that the spraying had little effect on the mosquitoes and was being done mainly for public relations—that is, to convince people that the city government was doing something about the epidemic.

The debate isn't easy to settle because the risks of spraying and the risks of the virus are both hard to measure and to compare. In 1999, when the West Nile virus killed seven people in the United States, it was easy to claim that the risk was so low that spraying mosquitoes was a bad idea. In 2002, the virus killed 188 people around the country. That's still less than one out of every one million people in the United States, but it's enough to make killing mosquitoes seem like a better idea.

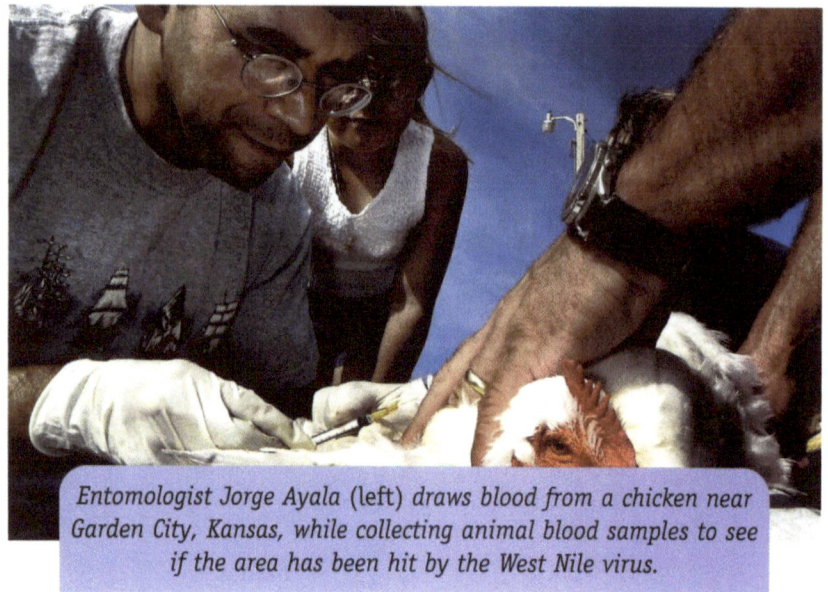
Entomologist Jorge Ayala (left) draws blood from a chicken near Garden City, Kansas, while collecting animal blood samples to see if the area has been hit by the West Nile virus.

Nile virus, the one in the United States most closely resembles one found in Israel between 1997 and 2000. This strain is especially deadly for birds. In Israel, large numbers of geese died from the West Nile virus. In America many species of birds, especially crows, have fallen victim to the virus. Animal experiments show that 100 percent of crows infected with this particular strain of the West Nile virus die.

The Mosquitoes

The West Nile virus has been found in fourteen different species of mosquito. It's most commonly found in two species, *Culex pipiens* (the common house mosquito) and *Culex restuans*. Since mosquitoes carry the West Nile virus, whatever affects the mosquito population affects the spread of the virus. Mosquitoes are active in the summer and fall, so the period from July to October is when outbreaks tend to occur. Mosquitoes die off in the winter, so a long severe winter will result in a smaller mosquito population the following summer, and, therefore, less danger posed by the West Nile virus. Mild winters increase the mosquito population and the danger from the virus. It's a bit less clear why hot, dry summers also seem to be associated with the West Nile virus—it may be that the evaporation of ponds into stagnant puddles creates an environment that helps mosquitoes breed.

Mosquito fish, pictured here, consume mosquito larvae and have been used to help control the spread of West Nile.

5

BATTLING THE VIRUS

Knowledge is the best defense we have against any epidemic. A great deal has been learned already about the West Nile virus. We know that it's a vector-borne disease. We know that it's found in a wide variety of species, and we know that it's carried to human beings by mosquitoes. We know a great deal about its chemistry. We have a test that recognizes antibodies of the virus in a blood sample (when we find these antibodies, we know the person has gotten the virus). We also have a test that can find the virus directly in a blood sample. We know from analyzing the virus's DNA exactly how it's related to similar viruses in the United States and around the world.

BATTLING THE VIRUS

But in their efforts to stop the West Nile virus, scientists and health workers are trying to find answers to a series of other questions. Where and when will the next outbreak of the West Nile virus occur? Can a quicker way of telling who has the West Nile virus be found (and thus, a quicker way of finding where the virus has struck)? Does it really help to kill mosquitoes, and how far should the spraying program go? How serious is the threat of the West Nile virus in comparison to threats from other illnesses? Is it going to taper off, with outbreaks becoming less frequent and less deadly as time goes on, or will it become worse?

Tracking the Spread of the Virus

Epidemiologists believe that killing virus-carrying mosquitoes may help slow the epidemic. But where are the virus-carrying mosquitoes? The first step toward finding the infected mosquitoes is finding where the virus is infecting people. Health-care workers and pest-control workers can then concentrate on killing the mosquitoes in that area. If this could be done early enough, the spread of the virus could be stopped. The mosquitoes would be dead, so they couldn't infect birds, and birds wouldn't carry the virus to other parts of the country.

A health department worker in Washington, D.C., holds a mosquito larvicide briquette, or "dunk," which was placed in mosquito breeding grounds throughout the area in the summer of 2002.

BATTLING THE VIRUS

Workers at the CDC keep in touch with hospitals all over the country and track every suspected case of West Nile fever. Blood samples are collected and brought to labs to confirm or disprove the presence of the virus. With the help of databases and computer modeling, the CDC uses this information to predict the spread of the virus.

Testing for the West Nile Virus

The problem is that by the time people start showing up in hospitals, sick with West Nile fever, the virus has already had many days to move on. CDC workers find themselves running to the place where the virus was, instead of where it is at the present time.

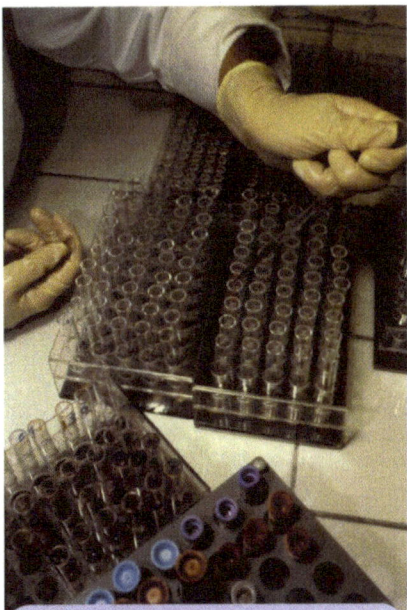

A lab technician draws blood from test tubes. The CDC relies on extensive blood testing to track the West Nile virus.

In fact, the standard tests for West Nile work only around fifteen days after the person has been infected. Like most tests for illness, they measure antibodies—the body's response to the virus—not the virus itself. It takes around fifteen days for the body to produce enough antibodies for the West Nile virus to be detected by a blood test. As a result, the test is not much use in fighting the epidemic.

One part of the solution is to develop a test that's quick and simple to do, which the CDC was working on as of August 2002. This will identify the virus itself and do it soon after a person has been infected. It's not clear yet how effective this will be.

When that test is perfected, though, the CDC will still face another obstacle: finding who to test it on. Since it takes a long time to come down with the symptoms of the West Nile virus, healthy people would have to be tested randomly. Blood tests aren't fun. People will put up with them only if they feel that the threat of the virus is serious.

Mosquito Surveillance

Another, and maybe better, way to check for the presence of the virus is to go directly to the mosquitoes. Entomologists—scientists who specialize in the study of insects—trap tens of thousands of mosquitoes and put them in coolers filled with dry ice. The mosquitoes are sorted into their different species, using what is

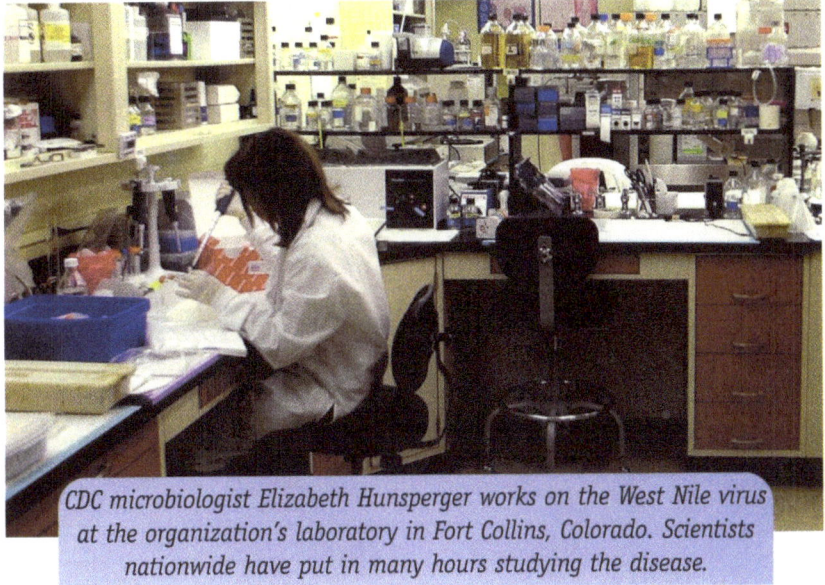

CDC microbiologist Elizabeth Hunsperger works on the West Nile virus at the organization's laboratory in Fort Collins, Colorado. Scientists nationwide have put in many hours studying the disease.

known about their distinct appearances, sometimes with the help of a microscope. It isn't practical to test individual mosquitoes for the virus, so researchers grind up fifty at a time and test them together.

Duane Gubler, director of the CDC's vector-borne infectious diseases division in Fort Collins, Colorado, suggests that understanding the behavior of mosquitoes is key to controlling the spread of the West Nile virus. We need to know how the mosquito population varies by season, where they breed, how they respond to rain and drought, and how we can tell in advance when their population is going to increase. "If we want to prevent these kinds of

Insect repellant sales soared by up to 50 percent at the Giant Eagle chain of supermarkets during the summer of 2002 as a result of the rising tide of West Nile infections throughout the nation.

outbreaks," says Gubler, "we need to get on with the business of developing effective mosquito surveillance and control programs. These diseases are very preventable in humans."

What Can We Do?

What can those of us who are not directly involved in public health do about the West Nile virus? The best thing to do, during the season when mosquitoes are active, is to avoid being bitten by them by using insect repellent when outdoors, wearing long-sleeved clothing, and staying indoors in the early evening

> **HOW SERIOUS IS THE THREAT OF WEST NILE FEVER?**
>
> In the summer of 2002, the West Nile virus was the big story in newspapers and on television news. But one question that arose was whether it deserved quite as much attention as it got. Should we be personally afraid of it? There are 250 million people in the United States, so the odds of dying from the West Nile virus are less than one in a million—the odds of getting a case severe enough to be reported to the CDC are around one in 74,000. These are still very slim odds.

when mosquitoes are most prone to bite. You can also eliminate standing water sources around your home. If you want to do more, the CDC recommends getting in touch with organized mosquito control programs, which exist in many areas.

GLOSSARY

bubonic plague An epidemic spread by rats and fleas that killed a third of the population of Europe in the 1300s.

clinic A medical facility where patients are treated on an outpatient basis, that is, without staying overnight.

Ebola A virus that occurs in Africa, in the Sudan and nearby areas of Zaire, causing an acute, fatal hemorrhagic fever in humans.

electron microscope An instrument that uses electrons to magnify tiny objects onto a fluorescent screen or photographic plate. It provides magnifications up to 1,000,000 times the actual size without loss of definition.

GLOSSARY

emergent virus   A virus that may have existed for a very long time in one small area and is now being found in new places.
encephalitis   Inflammation of the brain.
epidemic   A sudden, rapid spread of a disease.
epidemiologist   A scientist who studies the spread of disease.
flavivirus   A family of viruses to which St. Louis encephalitis and the West Nile virus belong.
HIV (human immunodeficiency virus)   The virus that causes the disease AIDS.
hot zone   A place where a virus is breeding in high concentration.
immune system   The bodily system that protects the body against foreign substances.
immunity   The ability to resist infection by a particular cause of disease.
lymph glands   Oval masses of tissue present in many places in the human body; they are part of the immune system and tend to become swollen during illness.
malathion   A type of insecticide.
meningitis   Inflammation of the membranes that envelop the brain and spinal cord.
myocarditis   Inflammation of the middle muscular layer of the heart wall.

outbreak A relatively sudden increase in the number of cases of a disease.

pathologist One who interprets and diagnoses the changes caused by disease in tissues and body fluids.

smallpox An acute contagious disease caused by a virus, characterized by fever, skin eruptions, and scar formation.

St. Louis encephalitis A virus that has been found in the United States since 1933. It is closely related to the West Nile virus.

transfusion The process of putting fluid into a vein or artery.

vaccine A preparation of killed or living microorganisms that is given to produce or artificially increase immunity to a particular disease.

vector-borne infectious disease An infectious disease that is carried to human beings through a carrier, often an insect. Some vector-borne diseases can also be spread person to person; others cannot.

virus A submicroscopic infective agent that is capable of growth and multiplication only in living cells.

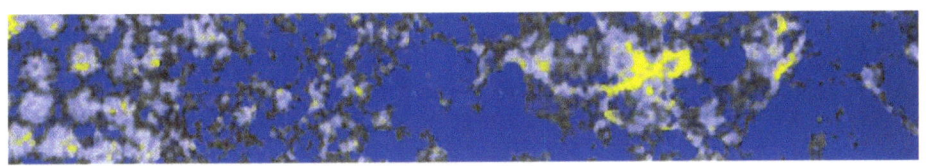

FOR MORE INFORMATION

Centers for Disease Control and Prevention (CDC)
CDC Disease Detectives
1600 Clifton Road
MS C-04
Atlanta, GA 30333
Web site: http://www.bam.gov/detectives

Centers for Disease Control and Prevention
Division of Vector-Borne Infectious Diseases
P.O. Box 2087
Fort Collins, CO 80522
(404) 639-3311
Web site: http://www.cdc.gov

National Institutes of Health
9000 Rockville Pike
Bethesda, MD 20892
(301) 496-4000
Web site: http://www.nih.gov

In Canada

Health Canada
West Nile Virus Surveillance Information
0904A Brooke Claxton Bldg.
Tunney's Pasture
Ottawa, ON K1A 0K9
(800) 267-1245
Web site: http://www.hc-sc.gc.ca/pphb-dgspsp/wnv-vwn

Web Sites

Due to the changing nature of Internet links, the Rosen Publishing Group, Inc., has developed an online list of Web sites related to the subject of this book. This site is updated regularly. Please use this link to access the list:

http://www.rosenlinks.com/epid/wenv

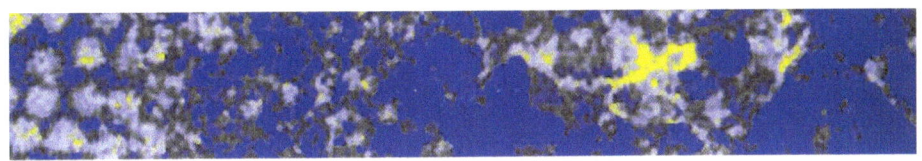

FOR FURTHER READING

Day, Nancy. *Malaria, West Nile, and Other Mosquito-Borne Diseases* (Diseases and People). New York: Enslow Publishers, Inc., 2001.

Despommier, Dickson, and Robert J. Demarest. *West Nile Story*. New York: Apple Trees Productions, 2001.

McGavin, George C., and Ken Preston-Mafham. *Bugs of the World*. New York: Blandford Press, 1999.

Peters, C. J., and Mark Olshaker. *Virus Hunter: Thirty Years of Battling Hot Viruses Around the World*. New York: Doubleday, 1998.

Spielman, Andrew, and Michael D'Antonio. *Mosquito: A Natural History of Our Most Persistent and Deadly Foe*. New York: Hyperion, 2001.

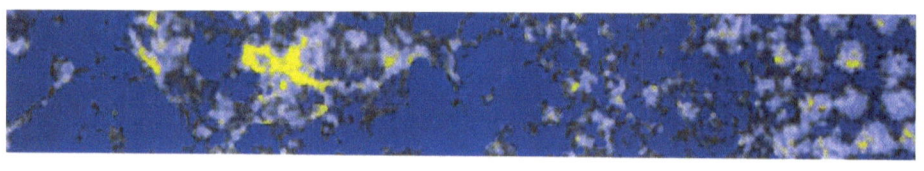

INDEX

A
Africa, 5, 15, 17–19, 41
Andresen, John, 28
anthrax, 11
antibodies, 40–41, 46, 50
Anvil (pesticide), 12
Asomoa, Kwame, 11
Aztecs, 6–7

B
birds, 9, 12, 18, 26–27, 29, 30, 33, 37, 44, 47
blood transfusions, 35–36
body aches, 13, 14
brain damage, 14
Bronx Zoo, 27
bubonic plague, 16
Buff, Ann, 11
Bunning, Mike, 10–11, 12

C
Centers for Disease Control and Prevention (CDC), 10, 16, 29, 30, 32, 33, 35, 37, 49, 50, 53
  Division of Vector-Borne Infectious Diseases, 10, 51
  "fever team," 10–12
Central America, 6–7
central nervous system, 21
Click, Ellie, 11

INDEX

E
encephalitis, 13–14, 18, 22, 27, 28, 29, 41
epidemic, 6, 7, 8, 12, 18, 21, 24, 28, 29, 32, 43, 47, 50
epidemiologists, 10–12, 21, 38

F
fever, 13, 14
flaviviruses, 41
Food and Drug Administration, 36
France, 18

G
Giuliani, Rudolph, 42
Gubler, Duane, 51–52

H
headache, 13, 14
HIV, 35, 41
hot zones, 12

I
immune system, 5–6, 40–41, 42
immunity, 5–6, 7, 12, 40–41
insects, 9, 16, 17
Israel, 18, 44

K
Kipp, Aaron, 11
Krueger, Judy, 11

L
Lancet, 24
Louisiana, 9–10, 33
lymph glands, 13

M
malathion (pesticide), 42
Marshall, Stacie, 11
meningitis, 13–14, 18, 22, 25
meningoencephalitis, 14, 18, 25
mosquitoes, 10, 16, 18, 20, 29, 35, 37, 44–45, 46, 47
  avoiding being bitten by, 30–31, 52–53
  breeding of, 19, 32, 33
  Culex pipiens species, 24, 45
  Culex restuans species, 45

locating, 11–12
spraying for, 29, 30, 33, 42–43, 47
studying, 50–52
myocarditis, 27

N
National Veterinary Services Laboratory, 26, 27
New York, 11, 26–32, 37, 42
New York City Department of Health and Mental Hygiene, 28, 42

P
pathologists, 26, 27
pesticides, 26, 29, 30, 33, 47
  debate over, 42–43
Petersen, Lyle R., 21

R
rash, 13
Roehrig, John T., 21
Romania, 5, 21–24, 25
Russia, 24–25

S
Slavinski, Sally, 38
sleeping sickness, 15, 17
Slidell Memorial Hospital, 10, 33
smallpox, 7
Smithburn, K. C., 17
South Africa, 18–19
St. Louis encephalitis, 28–29, 34–38, 41
Stone, Ward, 26–27

T
trypanosomiasis, African (sleeping sickness), 15

V
vaccines, 41
vector-borne infectious diseases, 15–17, 18, 41, 46
viruses
  about, 39–41
  emergent, 5–7
  vector-borne, 41

W
West Nile fever, 13, 23, 49

INDEX

West Nile virus
  in America, 5, 9–13, 14, 19, 21, 25, 26–38
  battling, 46–53
  deaths caused by, 9, 23, 25, 31, 32, 33, 43
  family/forms of, 41–44
  history of, 5, 15–25
  how it's contracted, 10, 12, 35–36, 46
  incubation period of, 12, 35
  spread of, 5, 12, 18, 20, 32
  symptoms of, 13–14
  testing for, 31, 46, 49–50
  in 2002, 32–34, 35, 43, 53

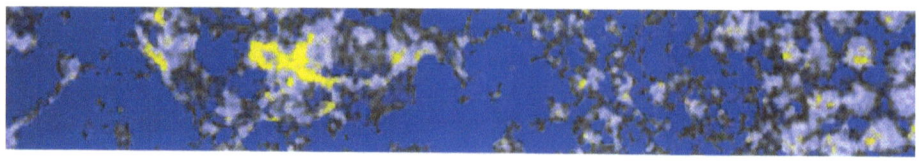

CREDITS

About the Author
Phillip Margulies is a freelance writer who lives in New York City.

Photo Credits
Cover and chapter title interior photos © NIH/Custom Medical Stock Photo, Inc.; p. 4 © Douglas Healey/AP/Wide World Photos; p. 11 © Harry Cabluck/AP/Wide World Photos; p. 13 © S. Fraser/Photo Researchers, Inc.; p. 16 © Tim Roske/AP/Wide World Photos; p. 19 © Bill Moffitt/*Roswell Daily Record*/AP/Wide World Photos; p. 20 © Wilfredo Lee/AP/Wide World Photos; p. 24 © Biophoto Associates/Photo Researchers, Inc.; p. 27 © David M. Jennings/The Image Works; p. 29 © Clint Keller/*Journal Gazette*/AP/Wide World Photos; pp. 30, 43 © Reuters NewMedia Inc./Corbis; p. 34 Tim Boyle/Getty Images; p. 36 © C. Todd Sherman/*Vicksburg Post*/AP/Wide World Photos; p. 44 © Brad Nading/*Garden City Telegram*/AP/Wide World Photos; p. 45 © Mark Crosse/*Fresno Bee*/AP/Wide World Photos; p. 48 © AFP/Corbis; p. 49 © SuperStock; p. 51 © Ed Andrieski/AP/Wide World Photos; p. 52 © Gary Tramontina/AP/Wide World Photos.

Designer: Evelyn Horovicz; Editor: Nicholas Croce

www.ingramcontent.com/pod-product-compliance
Lightning Source LLC
Chambersburg PA
CBHW041115070526
44584CB00002B/177